WORLD IN
FOCUS

FOCUS ON THE
United Kingdom

ALEX WOOLF

WORLD ALMANAC® LIBRARY

Please visit our web site at: www.worldalmanaclibrary.com
For a free color catalog describing World Almanac® Library's list of high-quality books
and multimedia programs, call 1-800-848-2928 (USA) or 1-800-387-3178 (Canada).
World Almanac® Library's fax: (414) 332-3567.

Library of Congress Cataloging-in-Publication Data

Woolf, Alex, 1964-
    Focus on the United Kingdom / by Alex Woolf.
        p. cm. — (World in focus)
    Includes bibliographical references and index.
    ISBN 0-8368-6724-6 (lib. bdg.)
    ISBN 0-8368-6731-9 (softcover)
    1. Great Britain—Juvenile literature. 2. Northern Ireland—Juvenile literature.
    I. Title. II. Series.
    DA27.5.W66 2006
    941—dc22   2006001927

This North American edition first published in 2007 by
World Almanac® Library
A Member of the WRC Media Family of Companies
330 West Olive Street, Suite 100
Milwaukee, WI 53212 USA

Commissioning editor: Victoria Brooker
Editor: Kelly Davis
Inside design: Chris Halls, www.mindseyedesign.co.uk
Cover design: Hodder Wayland
Series concept and project management by EASI-Educational Resourcing (info@easi-er.co.uk)
Statistical research: Anna Bowden
Maps and graphs: Martin Darlison, Encompass Graphics

World Almanac® Library editor: Gini Holland
World Almanac® Library cover design: Scott M. Krall

Picture acknowledgements:
The author and publisher would like to thank the following for allowing their pictures to be
reproduced in this publication: Easi-Images (Rob Bowden) cover, title page, 4, 5, 6, 12, 15, 16, 17,
19, 20, 23, 27, 29, 30, 33, 35, 38, 39, 41, 43, 48, 53, 54, 56, 57, 58; Easi-Images (Adrian Cooper)
44, 55; Corbis 9 (Archivo Iconografico, S.A.),10 (Gianni Dagli Orti), 13 (Bettmann), 18 (London
Aerial Photo Library), 21 (Richard Klune), 22 (Nic Bothma/Pool/Reuters), 24 (Yves Herman/
Reuters), 25 (Lewis Alan), 34, 36 (John Kolesidis), 37 (Reuters), 42 (Eleanor Bentall), 46
(Bettmann), 47 (Gideon Mendel), 49 (Ashley Cooper), 51 (Robert Paterson/Reuters) 59 (Stephen
Hird/Reuters); Chris Fairclough Worldwide/Chris Fairclough 8, 14, 26, 28, 40, 45, 50; Mary
Evans/Margaret Monck Photographs 11; Courtesy of Toyota (GB) Plc 31; Associated Ports'
Port of Southampton 32; Edward Parker 52.

The directional arrow portrayed on the map on page 7 provides only an approximation of north.
The data used to produce the graphics and data panels in this title were the latest available at the
time of production.

Printed in China

1 2 3 4 5 6 7 8 9 10 09 08 07 06

CONTENTS

Cover: The House of Parliament, in London, is where members of the House of Commons and House of Lords debate and pass the laws that govern the United Kingdom.

Title page: Visitors relax at the Bullring in Birmingham, with the Selfridges building behind them.

CHAPTER 1

The United Kingdom— An Overview

The United Kingdom of Great Britain and Northern Ireland (UK) is a nation on the British Isles of northwestern Europe, across the English channel from continental Europe. It consists of four political divisions—England, Scotland, Wales (which make up the island of Great Britain) and Northern Ireland (the northeastern part of the island of Ireland).

The UK's landscape offers rich variety. Much of Scotland and Wales display mountainous terrain punctuated by deep valleys, while most of England spreads out in plains checkered with fields and meadows. The UK is a land of ancient castles, stately homes, and small villages, as well as modern towns and cities.

A GLOBAL PLAYER

During the nineteenth and early twentieth centuries, the UK became the world's biggest economic and military power, when it controlled vast territories around the world (*see page 11*). The British Empire was the largest the world had ever seen, occupying a quarter of Earth's land surface and including about a quarter of the human race. The British spread their way of life, language, institutions, and traditions throughout their empire.

▼ The Welsh landscape is famous for its sharply rising hills and green valleys. Wales has three National Parks set up to protect the country's scenery and wildlife.

▲ London, the UK's capital city, contains a mixture of traditional and modern architecture, from the nineteenth-century Tower Bridge (*on the right*) to the recently built office buildings seen in the foreground.

Although it is no longer at the hub of an empire, the UK continues to play a highly influential role in global affairs. As head of the Commonwealth of Nations (an institution made up mostly of former colonies of the British Empire), it has maintained close economic and political relations with many of the countries it once ruled. The UK is one of only five permanent members of the United Nations (UN) Security Council, a founding member of the North Atlantic Treaty Organization (NATO), and a key nation in the European Union (EU).

Britain is also one of the richest countries in the world, with the fourth largest gross national product. By far, the largest proportion of its wealth is earned in the service sector, particularly banking, insurance, and business services. London, the capital city, is one of the world's leading financial and commercial centers.

NATIONAL CULTURE

Alongside its modern identity, the UK is also a country of deep-rooted traditions and a strong sense of its own history. For example, every year on November 5, the British people commemorate the foiling of a plot to blow up the British Parliament in 1605. Today, its monarch, although no longer politically powerful, remains an important national figurehead for many Britons, and a highly recognizable symbol of the UK around the world.

Since the 1960s, the UK has also become known worldwide for its popular culture, including

◀ Today, many British cities contain large communities of ethnic minorities. In Birmingham, shown here, around 22 percent of the population are of Afro-Caribbean or Asian origin.

from the Indian subcontinent, the Caribbean, and West Africa. This migration has added greatly to the UK's ethnic and cultural diversity, enriching all areas of British society, from music and the arts to business and politics.

These developments and many others throughout its history have made the UK the country it is today: outward looking, generally tolerant of other beliefs and cultures, yet also proud of its traditions.

Sometimes, the UK's role in international affairs can lead to problems. For example, the UK's traditionally close ties with the United States can lead to friction with its partners in the European Union, as in 2003, when the UK decided to take part in the U.S.-led invasion of Iraq. This invasion was strongly opposed by some countries in Europe, including France and Germany.

theater, film, television and popular music. Its greatest export, however, has been the English language, now spoken as a first or second language across a large part of the world.

A CHANGING SOCIETY

Throughout its history, the UK has experienced a long succession of invasions and migrations. This trend continued in the second half of the twentieth century, when the British government invited people from its former colonies to help with its rebuilding effort following World War II (1939–1945). In response, tens of thousands migrated to Britain

Physical geography

- ▷ Land area: 93,278 sq miles/241,590 sq km
- ▷ Water area: 1,247 sq miles/3,230 sq km
- ▷ Total area: 94,525 sq miles/244,820 sq km
- ▷ World rank (by area): 79
- ▷ Land boundaries: 224 miles/360 km
- ▷ Border countries: Ireland
- ▷ Coastline: 7,718 miles/12,429 km
- ▷ Highest point: Ben Nevis 4,406 feet/1,343 m
- ▷ Lowest point: The Fens -13 feet/-4 m

Source: CIA World Factbook

Legend

★ Capital
● Cities > 1,000,000
● Cities > 500,000
● Cities > 200,000
• other cities
▲ Mountain

Orkney Islands

Wick

North Sea

Outer Hebrides

NORTH WEST HIGHLANDS

Isle of Skye

Loch Ness

Inverness

GRAMPIAN MOUNTAINS

Aberdeen

SCOTLAND

Dundee

ATLANTIC OCEAN

Glasgow *Clyde*

Edinburgh

UNITED

SOUTHERN UPLANDS

Newcastle-upon-Tyne

Tyne

Sunderland

North Sea

Londonderry

NORTHERN

Lough Neagh

Belfast

IRELAND

Isle of Man

KINGDOM

Carlisle

LAKE DISTRICT

Tees

Middlesbrough

Irish Sea

Blackpool

York

Leeds

Ouse

Kingston upon Hull

IRELAND

Bradford

Bolton

Huddersfield

Liverpool

Manchester

Stockport

Sheffield

Bangor

P E N N I N E S

ENGLAND

Stoke-on-Trent

Derby

Nottingham

Trent

Norwich

CAMBRIAN MTNS

Wolverhampton

Walsall

Leicester

THE FENS

Dudley

Birmingham

Peterborough

Coventry

Northampton

Worcester

Cambridge

Ipswich

WALES

Cheltenham

Luton

Colchester

Gloucester

Oxford

Chelmsford

Severn

Swansea

Newport

Swindon

LONDON

Southend-on-Sea

Cardiff

Reading

Thames

Bristol

Bath

Canterbury

Crawley

Dover

ATLANTIC OCEAN

Southampton

Brighton & Hove

Exeter

Poole

Portsmouth

Eastbourne

Exe

Bournemouth

FRANCE

Plymouth

Penzance

English Channel

N

0   50   100 kilometres
0   50   100 miles

Shetland Islands

Mainland

Channel Islands

Alderney

Guernsey

FRANCE

Jersey

CHAPTER 2

History

For much of its history, the UK has been a target for invasion and settlement by people from many parts of the world. Successive waves of immigrants have left their mark on British culture, language, and beliefs and helped create the nation of the UK today. In turn, the British have explored, traded with, settled in, and dominated other countries around the globe.

ANCIENT BRITAIN

In about 6500 B.C., the glaciers that covered the British mainland melted, and the land bridge between Britain and France flooded to create the island of Great Britain. Archaeological evidence reveals that the early inhabitants of Britain comprised a varied group of people who had traveled from the European mainland. The population was small and scattered.

In about 4000 B.C., people brought knowledge of agriculture to Britain from Europe, ushering in the New Stone Age, or Neolithic Period. Neolithic people cleared large areas of forest for farmland. They mined flint, made pottery, and built Britain's first stone and wooden structures.

Metalworking arrived in Britain between about 3000 and 2500 B.C. Bronze tools and weapons gradually replaced flint and copper in about 2000 B.C.—the start of the Bronze Age. By 1400 B.C., Bronze Age people had built many circles of standing stones in Britain, including the famous Stonehenge in Wiltshire. The Iron Age began with the introduction of iron in about 700 B.C. Between 500 and 100 B.C., a people called the Celts from Central and Western Europe began to settle in Britain.

In 55 B.C., Roman general Julius Caesar invaded Britain. Caesar's stay was brief, but in A.D. 43, Roman commander Aulus Plautius successfully invaded, and the Romans took control of most of Britain (approximately the area of present-day England and Wales) for the next 400 years. On several occasions during the second and third centuries, the Romans advanced into Scotland, but never succeeded in absorbing it into their empire. The legacy of Roman rule includes a road network, towns such as London, Colchester, and York, and architecture—including Roman baths, such as those still at Bath—and the Latin language.

▼ Stonehenge is the most famous prehistoric monument in Britain. It was erected between 3000 and 1600 B.C., perhaps as a place of worship.

THE MIDDLE AGES

When the Roman legions withdrew in 410 A.D. —so that they could defend against attacks on other parts of their empire that were closer to Rome—Britain became vulnerable to attack from other invaders desiring territory and resources. Britons were attacked from the north by a people known as the Picts and from Ireland by a people called the Scots. In the mid-400s, Angles, Jutes, and Saxons from Germany invaded, driving native Britons to the western fringes of Britain—Wales and Cornwall. The Anglo-Saxons, as they became known, occupied what would become England and Wales. They established several independent kingdoms.

From 787, Vikings from Scandinavia began a wave of invasions, eventually conquering every kingdom on the island except Wessex in the southwest. In 828, the powerful Wessex king Egbert became the first king of all England. The country did not stay united for long, however. In 830, the kingdom of Mercia in the Midlands reestablished its independence, and it was not until Athelstan's reign (924–939) that England became permanently unified.

In 1066, William, Duke of Normandy (a province of France), conquered England. William installed a new ruling class and introduced Norman systems of law and administration. The king offered land to his barons in exchange for military service in a system known as feudalism. French replaced English as the official language.

Focus on: Magna Carta

Most of the kings who ruled England after the Norman Conquest treated their barons fairly and respected the traditions of feudalism. King John (1199–1216), however, ruled without consulting his barons. He demanded more money and services from them than earlier kings. When John lost a war with France, the barons rebelled, and in 1215, they forced him to sign a document, known as the Magna Carta (Great Charter), which limited royal power and made it clear that even the king was not above the law. The Magna Carta was an important step forward in the development of democracy in Britain.

▶ This detail from the Bayeux Tapestry, created to celebrate the Norman victory at the Battle of Hastings in 1066, shows the last time Britain was successfully invaded and conquered by a foreign power, the French of Normandy.

The Normans continued to rule Britain until the twelfth century, when a civil war led to the rise of the Plantagenet dynasty, a powerful French family that ruled Britain from 1154 to 1485.

From 1337 to 1453, England and France fought an intermittent conflict, known as the Hundred Years' War, over the right to control certain territories in France. England lost most of its French lands and declined into a period of civil war called the Wars of the Roses (1455-1485), when the branches of the Plantagenet dynasty, the houses of York and Lancaster, fought for the English crown (the right to be king).

THE TUDORS AND STUARTS

The Wars of the Roses ended with the defeat of the Yorkist king Richard III by the Lancastrian Henry Tudor, who became Henry VII. Under the rule of his son, Henry VIII, England began to reject the Catholic religion and Wales was annexed to England (1536–1543).

Later in the sixteenth century, England grew as an economic and military power. English explorers, such as Sir Francis Drake, traversed the oceans, and English culture enjoyed a flowering of literature with the works of Shakespeare, Marlowe, and Spenser. In 1588,

Philip II of Spain sent a fleet called the Armada to try to conquer England and return it to Catholicism, but it was defeated by the English.

▲ Henry VIII married six times during his reign. He finally succeeded in his desire for a son when his third wife, Jane Seymour, gave birth to Edward in 1536. Henry's most successful heir, however, would be his daughter Elizabeth.

Focus on: The English Reformation

In the early 16th century, a movement began in Europe known as the Protestant Reformation, which rejected the authority of the Pope in Rome. In England, Protestantism was greatly helped by Henry VIII's decision to break with the Catholic Church. Henry did this because his desire for a male heir led him to divorce his wife Catherine and marry his lover, Anne Boleyn—which the Pope would not agree to. By making himself supreme leader of the English Church and removing the Pope's authority in his kingdom, Henry played a major part in the rise of the Protestant Church in England. The English Reformation was completed under the rule of his daughter, Elizabeth I (1558–1603), when Protestantism became the official religion of England.

In the seventeenth century, a power struggle between the Crown and Parliament culminated in a civil war (1642–1649). Oliver Cromwell, second in command of the Parliamentary forces, defeated the king's forces, and parliament established the republic known as the Commonwealth, which had no monarch. Although the monarchy was restored in 1660, parliament held onto most of its newly won powers. In 1707, the kingdoms of England and Scotland became joined in the Act of Union. The new nation was known from then on as Great Britain.

In 1607, James I of England confiscated lands belonging to the Catholic nobility in the north of Ireland (Ulster) and began to encourage Scottish Protestants to settle there. He believed that this "plantation of Ulster" would prevent future rebellions in Ireland, and gradually win the population over to Protestantism. Over the next ninety years, well over 100,000 Scottish Protestants settled in Ulster, establishing Protestantism as the dominant religion there.

THE 1700S AND 1800S

In the 1700s, Great Britain developed a more modern system of government with political parties and an appointed team of ministers, led by a prime minister, to represent the king in parliament. Britain created colonies in India, the Americas, and Australia, which opened up new opportunities for trade. In 1801, Great Britain annexed Ireland to form the United Kingdom. Under Queen Victoria (1837–1901), the British Empire reached its height.

▲ Passengers from a British ship disembark in colonial India in 1916.

Focus on: The Industrial Revolution

Between 1740 and 1850, Britain underwent a period of remarkable economic and social transformation known as the Industrial Revolution. Power-driven machines replaced manual labor in many industries, and giant factories replaced homes and workshops as centers of manufacturing. Large numbers of people moved from the country to the towns in search of work. Industrial output reached new heights in the nineteenth century, and the country became known as "the workshop of the world." Rapid industrialization also created an urban underclass who lived and worked in appalling conditions. Pressure for reform from campaigners such as William and Catherine Booth (who tried to improve the working conditions of women), Elizabeth Gaskell (a novelist who wrote about urban poverty), and Robert Owen (a factory reformer) led to a series of laws that improved conditions for many. For example, a series of Factory Acts beginning in 1833 reduced the working hours and improved the working conditions of women and children employed in factories. The Mines Act of 1842 banned employment of women and children underground.

◀ The Iron Bridge, built over the Severn River in Shropshire in 1779, was the world's first iron bridge. The local area, known as Ironbridge Gorge, is regarded as the birthplace of the Industrial Revolution, and is a major center of Britain's industrial heritage.

LOSS OF EMPIRE

By the early 1900s, Britain was the richest and most powerful nation in the world. However, World War I (1914–18) cost Britain the lives of 750,000 servicemen and severely weakened the UK economy. The war was fought between the Allies (Britain, France, the U.S., and others) and the Central Powers (including Germany, Austria-Hungary, the Ottoman Empire, and others). Caused mainly by economic and political rivalry, the war was won by the Allies.

From 1910, a movement grew for Irish independence, resisted fiercely by Protestants in the north. This led to a partition of Ireland in 1921, with the south forming the Irish Free State and the northern province of Ulster remaining part of the UK.

Britain played a major part in the Allied victory in World War II (1939–45), but the war devastated the country's economy and left many of its cities in ruins. Lacking the resources to keep control of its colonies, Britain gave in to increasing demands for independence from India and countries in Africa, the Caribbean, and elsewhere. Having lost its empire, Britain sought a new global role as a founding member of NATO (North Atlantic Treaty Organization), an alliance formed to counter the threat of the Union of Soviet Socialist Republics (USSR) during the Cold War (1945–90). From 1973, it has been a member of the European Economic Community (EEC), and it joined the European Union (EU) in 1993.

WELFARE AND GIVING UP POWER

At home, the elected Labour government of 1945–51 created a welfare state, including the National Health Service and a social security system that looked after all citizens "from cradle to grave." Major industries were nationalized. Under the Conservative governments of 1979–1997, government involvement in citizens' lives was reduced and taxes were lowered.

Since 1997, the UK government has devolved (transferred) some of its powers to new assemblies in Scotland and Wales. In Northern Ireland, prolonged, centuries-long conflict between the republicans (supporting a united Ireland) and the loyalists (supporting Northern Ireland remaining part of the UK) was partly resolved in a 1998 political settlement in which powers were devolved to a Northern Ireland Assembly. This settlement appeared to bring an end to a thirty-year campaign of terrorism by the Provisional IRA (Irish Republican Army), a

▲ Winston Churchill tours the ruins of Coventry Cathedral following a German air raid. Over 30,000 Britons were killed in bomb attacks during 1940 and 1941.

terrorist organization dedicated to the removal of British forces from Northern Ireland and the establishment of a united Ireland. As well as attacking British military and Ulster police targets in Northern Ireland, the IRA set off bombs and carried out kidnappings and assassinations in mainland Britain. In 2005, the IRA announced the end of its armed struggle.

In recent years, Britain has actively supported American foreign policy in the war against terrorism and joined the United States in military attacks against Afghanistan in 2001–2002 and Iraq in 2003. The invasion of Iraq was opposed by many people in Britain and led to large-scale anti-war demonstrations.

CHAPTER 3

Landscape and Climate

The UK covers an area of 94,248 sq miles (244,820 sq km), of which 1,911 sq miles (3,230 sq km) is covered with water in the form of lakes, rivers, and streams. For a relatively small country, the UK has a great diversity of landscapes, from the mountains and valleys of Scotland and Wales to the gentle hills and lowlands of England.

THE NORTH

Britain's highest mountain, Ben Nevis, 4,408 feet (1,343 m), dominates the Scottish Highlands that make up most of northern Scotland. South of the Scottish Highlands rolls a gentle plain called the Central Lowlands. The Southern Uplands, a region of low, rounded hills, lie south of the Central Lowlands, and mark the border between Scotland and England. The Cambrian Mountains cover most of Wales and include Wales's highest peak, Mount Snowdon, at 3,560 feet (1,085 m). The south of Wales is mostly plateau, cut through by deep river valleys. The north of England is dominated by the Pennines, an upland region known as the "backbone of England" that stretches from the Scottish border southward to Sheffield. Northern Ireland's landscape is generally lower but it has a chain of highland peaks known as the Mountains of Mourne.

THE SOUTH

South of the Pennines, the rest of England and eastern Wales is made up of lowlands. These gently rolling plains are occasionally interrupted by low hills and ridges such as the Mendips near Bristol and the South Downs along the south coast between Southampton and Eastbourne. The Fens of East Anglia and the Somerset Levels are particularly low areas, dominated by wetlands and marshes. The land

◀ The Great Glen in the Scottish Highlands formed millions of years ago. This rugged valley is 73 miles (117 km) long and contains three freshwater lakes.

here is very fertile and, to take advantage of this, a large proportion of wetland has been drained to create farmland.

 Tourists on a ship on the Mersey River spot Liverpool's so-called Three Graces—the Royal Liver Building, the Cunard Building, and Customs House.

RIVERS

Many of the UK's rivers have wide mouths, called estuaries, up which ocean tides flow. These include the Thames, Mersey, Humber, Severn, Clyde, and Forth. The estuaries provide excellent harbors, and the cities on these rivers are all important ports. These include London (Thames), Bristol (Severn), and Glasgow (Clyde).

Did you know?

The lowest point in the island of Great Britain is in the Fens, near Ely. It ranges from sea level to 15 feet (4.6 m) below sea level, depending on the tide of the North Sea.

COASTS AND ISLANDS

The UK's highly varied coastline includes cliffs, mudflats, rocky beaches, salt marshes, sand dunes, sandy beaches, and fishing towns nestling in sheltered bays. Off Britain's coasts are a number of small islands which are all part of the UK. These include Anglesey, off the

Did you know?

The UK's largest lake is Lough Neagh in Northern Ireland. It is about 18 miles (29 km) long and 15 miles (24 km) wide at its widest point, and covers about 150 sq miles (388 sq km).

northwest coast of Wales; the Isle of Wight, off England's southern coast; the Outer Hebrides, an archipelago of islands off the west coast of Scotland; the Orkney Islands, to the northeast of Scotland; and the Shetland Islands, about 100 miles (160 km) north of Scotland. The UK also has several dependencies close to its shores, including the Isle of Man in the Irish Sea and the Channel Islands off the northern coast of France. These dependencies are not part of the UK, but have a very close relationship with it.

A TEMPERATE CLIMATE

The UK has a mild climate, influenced by wind and ocean currents, which help prevent the extremes of heat and cold that may be experienced by other places of a similar latitude, such as Labrador in North America. The main

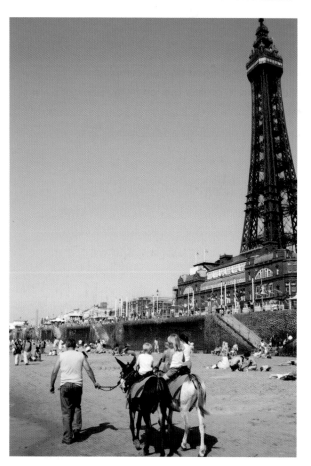

cause of the UK's mild temperatures is the Gulf Stream, a warm ocean current that sweeps up from the equator and flows past the British Isles. Southwesterly winds blow across this current and keep winter temperatures around 18 °F (10 °C) higher than they would otherwise be. As a result, winter temperatures seldom drop lower than 10 °F (-12 °C).

In the summer, the ocean is cooler than the land, and winds blowing in from the sea prevent high temperatures on land, which rarely exceed 90 °F (32 °C). Scotland and northern England are generally cooler than the UK average, and can be affected by cool Arctic air from the North Pole. The southeast of England is generally warmer than the rest of England and benefits from warm continental air traveling north from mainland Europe.

A LAND OF RAIN

The sea winds also bring plenty of rain. In general, western regions are considerably wetter than eastern areas. Highland areas are also wetter than lowlands, and above 2,000 feet (600 m), average annual precipitation is around 60 inches (1,500 mm) and can be as high as 200 inches (5,100 mm). This rainfall compares to a UK average of around 40 inches (1,000 mm). The driest area is southeastern England, parts of which receive less than 20 inches (510 mm) per year. The rain generally falls as a light, steady drizzle, and is fairly evenly distributed through the year, giving Britain the reputation as a land of seemingly constant rainfall. In fact, it often has days of mixed sun and rain.

◀ Vacationers enjoy the beach at the resort town of Blackpool in Lancashire. Above them, the famous Blackpool Tower soars to a height of 518 feet (158 meters).

Focus On: Climate Change

The 1990s was the warmest and driest decade in the UK since records began in 1860. Experts have warned that this may be evidence of climate change caused by increased carbon dioxide emissions due to human consumption of fossil fuels. In the UK, climate change is expected to increase average temperatures by 1.8–8.1 °F (1–4.5 °C) by 2100, with the greatest changes felt in the south of England. Rainfall patterns are also expected to change, with drier summers and wetter winters. In the south of England, precipitation may be reduced by up to 50 percent, forcing farmers to consider growing crops more suited to a drier, Mediterranean climate, such as grapes and peppers. Winter storms are also likely to increase, and flooding could become a regular problem for up to two million people in the UK by 2050.

▲ The Thames flood barrier, completed in 1984, is designed to protect London from flooding. During storms or high tides, huge steel gates are raised from the river bed, forming a wall across the river.

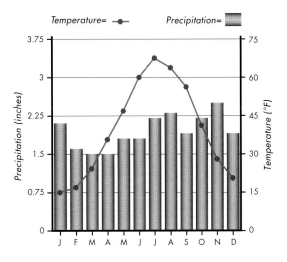

▲ Average monthly climate conditions in London.

CHAPTER 4

Population and Settlements

For its size, the UK supports a large population. In 2005, 59.6 million people gave the UK a population density of around 230 people per 628 sq miles (sq km). This is more than double the population density of France and nearly eight times that of the U.S.

AN URBAN NATION

The landscape has influenced where people have settled. A large majority of the population (84 percent) live on the generally flatter and larger land of England. Scotland is home to 8 percent of the British people, while another 5 percent live in Wales and 3 percent in Northern Ireland.

The majority, 89 percent, of the British people live in towns and cities. About one third of the British live in one of England's seven metropolitan areas. These are Greater London, Greater Manchester, Merseyside, South Yorkshire, Tyne and Wear, West Midlands, and West Yorkshire. The largest cities are London (7.6 million), Birmingham and Manchester (both 2.2 million), and Leeds (1.4 million).

AN AGING POPULATION

People in the UK are, on average, living longer, studying longer, marrying later, and having fewer children than previous generations. These social trends, combined with improvements in health care and education, have given the UK a declining and aging population. The proportion of young people (0–14 years), for example, fell from 23.3 percent of the population in 1960 to 18.1 percent in 2003. Over the same time period,

► This aerial view shows a residential area of Birmingham in the West Midlands. Like many British cities, Birmingham's population expanded rapidly in the twentieth century, and it is now the UK's second largest city.

the proportion of the population above retirement age (65 years) increased from 11.7 percent to 16 percent. If this trend to aging population continues, it is likely to lead to social problems, because the government will need to increase taxes to pay for the larger numbers of retired people. The increase in older people may also affect the pensions industry—an estimated 12 million people in the UK are not saving

enough toward their retirement. To deal with this concern, the government plans to increase the retirement age from 60 to 65.

▼ Elderly women often enjoy a day out at such attractions as Norwich Cathedral. With rising numbers of people over the age of 65, the "gray money," or spending power of retired people, has become a significant force in the UK economy.

Focus on: London

The capital city of the United Kingdom is one of the world's oldest cities. It began as two cities—the City of London, founded by the Romans in A.D. 43, and the City of Westminster, established about 1,000 years later. Today, Greater London is the UK's most urbanized area. With 7.6 million residents, it is home to about an eighth of the UK's population and is the most populated city

in Europe. Always a cosmopolitan city, it has attracted people from many parts of the British Commonwealth and elsewhere so that today, nearly one third of London's population comes from overseas, giving the city a rich and diverse culture. Rich in history and home to Buckingham Palace as well as incredible museums and theater, London is also a favorite tourist attraction.

ETHNIC DIVERSITY

Since the 1950s, the population of the UK has become increasingly multiethnic. This trend, however, should not be exaggerated. According to the UK census (2001), ethnic minority groups accounted for less than 6 percent of the total population. The largest ethnic minorities are those coming from the Caribbean and Africa (875,000 people), India (840,255 people), and Pakistan and Bangladesh (639,390 people). Substantial numbers of Americans, Australians, and Chinese, as well as Europeans, also make the UK their home. The UK's immigrant population is concentrated mostly in areas of the inner city (the central parts of cities) and more than half live in Greater London.

CITY AND COUNTRY

Since the 1950s, many of the UK's inner cities, which rose to greatness during the Industrial Revolution, have grown poorer. Problems include a lack of jobs, poor housing, and rising crime. Advances in transportation have made it much easier for people to live in the suburbs and work in the city. Inner-city populations fell as people moved out to the suburbs.

In 1988, the government launched a campaign to revive inner cities. They established "Enterprise Zones" in cities such as Cardiff, Belfast, Glasgow, and Liverpool, and offered tax incentives to new businesses willing to invest. Some regeneration plans have improved inner-city life, although many deprived and crime-ridden neighborhoods still exist.

 Did you know?

Immigration may be crucial to the UK's future prosperity. The combined effects of emigration from the UK, a declining birth rate, and increased longevity mean that by 2025, the UK will need 10 million new immigrants of working age to allow the nation to maintain its current levels of wealth and productivity.

▶ A street festival in Stoke on Trent in the West Midlands celebrates the multicultural nature of the region. The largest ethnic minority populations in the West Midlands originate from India, Pakistan, and the Caribbean.

The exodus from the inner cities has changed the complexion of the UK's rural communities, which were once dominated by farming. Many villages now contain more city commuters than full-time farmers. The countryside has also proved attractive to retired city workers, and in places like Cornwall, Devon, East and West Sussex, and parts of Wales, more than a fifth of the population is over retirement age. In recent decades, the beauty and variety of the English countryside has proved a magnet for tourists, and many residents of rural communities now work in the tourist industry.

disproportionately high demand for housing in London and the southeast, due to the increasing number of jobs in this region. In London alone, the demand for housing grows by an estimated 90,000 every year.

HOUSING

In recent years, various social trends have led to housing shortages in parts of the UK. Increasing divorce rates and a greater number of single-person households have caused a rise in single-occupancy housing, from 14 percent in 1961 to 29 percent in 2001. Another trend has been the

▲ Newcastle, in the northeast of England, has enjoyed substantial redevelopment of its Quayside. This formerly declining inner city area is becoming a major center of tourism and leisure.

Population data

- Population: 59.4 million
- Population 0–14 years: 18%
- Population 15–64 years: 66%
- Population 65+ years: 16%
- Population growth rate: 0.3%
- Population density:
  628.4 per sq mile/242.6 per sq km
- Urban population: 89%
- Major cities: London 7,615,000
  Birmingham 2,215,000
  Manchester 2,193,000

Source: United Nations and World Bank

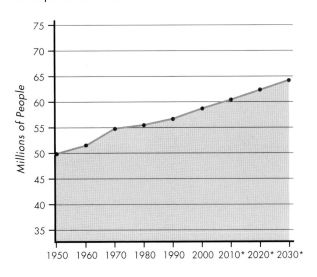

* Projected Population

▲ Population growth 1950–2030

CHAPTER 5

Government and Politics

The UK is a constitutional monarchy, which means that the head of state is the king or queen, ruling to the extent allowed by the various documents and customs that make up its constitution. In fact, since the early eighteenth century, the monarch's role has been largely ceremonial, and political power actually rests with the prime minister and the cabinet. The prime minister is a member of parliament (MP) and the leader of the largest political party in the House of Commons, which is the elected chamber of parliament. The cabinet is made up of MPs from the majority party, appointed by the prime minister to head the various departments of state, such as the Treasury and the Home Office.

PARLIAMENT

The prime minister and the cabinet initiate policy. Only parliament has the power to make new laws. The UK parliament is made up of two chambers, the House of Commons and the House of Lords. The House of Commons is composed of elected MPs, each of which represents a constituency in the country. The House of Lords is made up of peers (members of the noble class) who have either inherited their position or been appointed to it. The

▼ Queen Elizabeth II visited Nigeria in 2003. One of the Queen's roles as head of state is to represent Britain on state visits to other countries and on ceremonial occasions.

House of Commons is the more powerful of the two chambers. Since 1911, the House of Lords has only had the power to delay legislation.

▲ In the Houses of Parliament in London, members of the House of Commons and House of Lords debate and pass the laws that govern the UK.

THE ELECTORAL SYSTEM

Since the late seventeenth century, the UK has had a two-party system. Since the 1920s, the dominant parties have been the Conservative and Labour parties. Smaller parties, such as the Liberal Democrats and Scottish and Welsh nationalist parties, have only managed to gain relatively limited representation in parliament. This is because the electoral system that operates in the UK, known as "first-past-the-post," tends to favor larger parties. Under this system, candidates with the most votes win. There are no prizes for coming second. There have been calls by organizations such as the Electoral Reform Society and the Liberal Democratic Party to reform the UK electoral system so that it more fairly reflects actual voting patterns across the country and includes some minority parties. First-past-the-post does have the advantage, according to its supporters, of producing firm and decisive government.

Focus on: The UK's "Unwritten Constitution"

A constitution is a set of rules that govern a country's political behavior. British government evolved in a rather haphazard way over many centuries, and, as a result, its constitution is not a clear set of rules laid down in a single document, such as in France or the U.S. Instead, the British constitution is made up of a range of historical customs, laws, and conventions.

HANDING OVER POWER

In 1999, the UK government handed over certain powers to newly set up national assemblies in its regions of Scotland, Wales, and Northern Ireland. The Scottish Parliament has powers over areas such as education, health, housing, transportation, the environment, and agriculture, while the central government of the UK retains control of foreign affairs, defense, and economic policy. The Welsh assembly is much less powerful than the Scottish Parliament, because it lacks the power to make new laws or gather taxes. The Northern Ireland assembly was granted limited executive and legislative powers but was dissolved in 2002 following a breakdown in the peace process, and direct rule from the UK was reimposed.

LOCAL GOVERNMENT

Most everyday services in the UK are controlled and maintained by local authorities. These include roads, parks, libraries, schools, street cleaning, fire fighting, social services, and garbage collection. Local governments have few law-making powers and must act within the laws laid down by parliament, but they do have the power to raise property taxes, which amount to about a quarter of all the tax revenues raised in the UK.

elected assembly, with responsibility for public transportation, policing, emergency services, the environment, and planning. If the office of mayor is seen as a success, other UK cities may also get the chance to elect their own mayor.

THE EUROPEAN UNION

The UK's membership in the EU has been a cause of controversy in recent years. The EU began as the EEC (European Economic Community), an alliance of European nations to promote free trade in Europe. The EU has since developed powerful institutions of its own, such as the European Parliament and a Court of Justice. It also has its own economic and social policy and the beginnings of a

Most cities are run by metropolitan councils made up of elected members. London has its own separate structure of government, with thirty-two boroughs. In 2000, London gained its first directly elected mayor, together with an

▲ UK Prime Minister Tony Blair (*center*) meets with the presidents of the European Union and European Parliament at a summit of EU heads of state. Many Britons remain skeptical about the benefits of closer integration with other European states.

foreign policy. The EU is beginning to resemble a nation in its own right, and the UK, like other member nations, is obliged to accept the EU's decisions. Many in the UK fear that these developments threaten the sovereignty (independent authority) of the UK parliament.

Did you know?

The UK has a total of 468 local authorities and 26,000 elected councillors. Over two million people are employed in local government in the UK.

Focus on: Northern Ireland

In 1922, when Ireland gained its independence from the UK, six of the northern counties, known collectively as Northern Ireland or Ulster, decided to remain a part of the UK. The people of Northern Ireland have long been divided on political and religious lines. The majority are Protestants. Most of these are unionists, which means they wish to remain a part of the UK. A strong minority of the population are Catholic (as are most people in the Republic of Ireland to the south). Most Catholics are nationalists, or Republicans, who support the reunification of

Ireland. Conflict between the unionists and nationalists broke out in the late 1960s. A peace process began in 1994, leading, in 1998, to a peace agreement. A power-sharing legislature called the Northern Ireland Assembly was established in 1999. Continued political conflict, however, led the British government to suspend the assembly. In 2005, the Republican terrorist group, IRA, agreed to end the armed struggle and support the political process, and the UK government responded by reducing the number of troops it had stationed in Northern Ireland.

▶ Riot police take cover as unionist protesters throw missiles and set a roadblock on fire in Belfast in July 2000. Despite progress toward peace, a simmering mistrust remains between the two communities in Northern Ireland, which can sometimes explode into violence.

CHAPTER 6

Energy and Resources

The UK has larger energy resources—including coal, oil, and natural gas—than any other member of the EU. It has plenty of good agricultural land and forests and is one of Europe's leading fishing nations. The UK also benefits from reasonable reserves of minerals.

FOSSIL FUELS

The UK coal industry has been declining steadily for the past 100 years. Since its peak year of 1913, when 300 million tons (305 million tonnes) were produced, output has fallen by more than 80 percent. During the 1980s, many coal mines were closed because they were no longer economical to run, and it was cheaper to import energy resources from other countries.

The discovery of oil in the North Sea in the 1960s, and its subsequent exploitation from the mid-1970s, have greatly boosted Britain's energy supplies. The UK's North Sea oil fields produce an average output of nearly three million barrels per day.

Natural gas from the North Sea began to be available in large quantities from 1967. A national network of pipelines has been built, and, in 2001, it contributed toward 40 percent of the UK's total energy consumption, compared to 32 percent from oil and 17 percent from coal. Estimates suggest the North Sea reserves of oil and gas are likely to start running low between 2020 and 2030. Long before then, the UK will need to start importing these resources in larger quantities to fulfill the UK's energy requirements.

ALTERNATIVE ENERGY SOURCES

Burning fossil fuels (coal, oil, and gas) causes carbon dioxide emissions, which pollute the atmosphere and add to global warming. These fuels are not renewable. Using fossil fuels is therefore not a sustainable policy in the long run, and alternatives must be found. In 1997, the UK signed the Kyoto Protocol, an

◀ Men work at an oil rig in the North Sea. Production of North Sea oil has declined steadily since its peak in 1999.

international agreement which commits many nations to reducing carbon dioxide emissions by cutting down on energy consumption and looking at alternative energy sources.

One alternative is nuclear energy. The UK has twelve nuclear power stations which together supply around 23 percent of the country's electricity. Nuclear energy, however, also has its drawbacks: an accident at a nuclear plant can cause a major environmental disaster and the waste produced is very dangerous, difficult to dispose of, and, even when carefully disposed of, remains dangerously radioactive for thousands of years.

▲ The UK currently has 136 wind farms and plans to build many more. Although a source of clean, renewable energy, critics complain that wind farms are noisy and spoil the look of the environment.

? Did you know?

The world's first large-scale nuclear power station was opened in 1956 at Calder Hall, Cumbria, in northwest England.

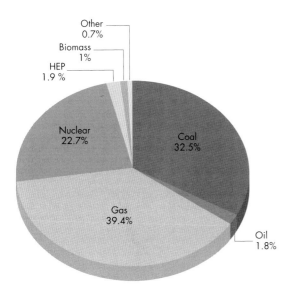

Other
0.7%

Biomass
1%

HEP
1.9%

Nuclear
22.7%

Coal
32.5%

Gas
39.4%

Oil
1.8%

▲ Electricity production by type

Energy Data

🗁 Energy consumption as % of world total: 2.4

🗁 Energy consumption by sector (% of total):

Industry:	26.1
Transportation:	32.3
Agriculture:	0.8
Services:	10.5
Residential and other:	30.3

🗁 CO_2 emissions as % of world total: 2.3

🗁 CO_2 emissions per person per year: 9.92 tons/9 tonnes

Source: World Resources Institute

Other alternatives include non-polluting, renewable energy sources such as biomass (any organic material that can be converted into a source of energy), wind, wave, tidal, and solar power. In 2005, approximately 3.6 percent of electricity in the UK came from renewable sources. The government has given targets to electricity suppliers to increase the percentage of electricity they supply from renewable sources to 10.4 percent by 2011.

AGRICULTURE AND FORESTRY

Approximately 75 percent of UK land is used for agriculture. The most important crops are wheat, barley, oats, sugar beets, potatoes, or rapeseed (which is used to make vegetable oil, livestock feed, and industrial lubricant). The main kinds of livestock are cattle, sheep, pigs, and poultry. The UK imports about a third of its food supply. Imports include bananas, citrus fruits, peppers, pineapples, sugar, and other foods not easily grown in the UK's climate. As a member of the EU, UK agricultural policy conforms to the EU's Common Agricultural Policy (CAP). The CAP offers farmers a stable income by providing a system of minimum prices for their products and offering subsidies so that their goods are competitive on world markets. British governments have criticized the CAP because UK farmers receive less financial help from the CAP than British taxpayers pay into it (because the UK has a smaller farming sector than other European countries). Many in the UK feel that their taxes are supporting inefficient European farmers.

About 10 percent of UK land is devoted to forestry. British forests produce nearly 30 million cubic feet (9 million cubic meters)

◀ Jersey cows go out to pasture at a dairy farm in Hampshire. The number of dairy farms in the UK fell by 46 percent between 1985 and 2003. Dairy farmers are finding it increasingly difficult to make a profit from milk production.

of wood each year. This wood provides the country with only about 15 percent of its annual timber requirements. Most of the UK's imported wood comes from producers in Europe and North and South America.

FISHING

Living on an island surrounded by sea, fishing has naturally always been important to the people of the UK. The most popular local fish are cod, haddock, mackerel, herring, whiting, and plaice, as well as various kinds of shellfish. Fish farms produce salmon, trout, and shellfish. In total, the UK fishing industry catches around 840,000 tons (853,000 tonnes) of fish annually. The industry, however, has been in decline for some years due to overfishing, which caused depleted fish stocks, especially of cod. Under EU rules, the UK has had to limit the amount of fish it can catch within British waters, as these seas are also fished by other member nations. The UK fishing industry now supplies only about half the UK's total demand.

MINERALS

Metals mined in the UK include tin and zinc. Its most valuable minerals, however, are non-metallic, and include sand, gravel, and limestone, which are quarried for use in the construction industry. Chalk, used for making cement, is found in large quantities in southeast England. Other minerals include slate, talc, dolomite, barite, celestite, sandstone, gypsum, and various types of clay. The southwest peninsula is known for its kaolin, or china clay, used to make pottery.

Focus on: Water Resources

Despite receiving plenty of rainfall, the UK has fairly limited water resources and frequently faces water shortages, particularly during the summer months. Summer rainfall does not help the water supply because the ground is too hard to absorb the rain and refill the reservoirs. Winter rain is often so heavy that it does not soak in, but saturates the topsoil and then runs off into rivers. For its size, the UK is also a big consumer of water, at 157.5 quarts (150 liters) per person per day. Another problem is water leakage. Broken and leaking pipes lose about 3,170,064,615 quarts (three billion liters) of water each day .

▲ During dry spells in the summer months, water levels in British reservoirs can often sink dangerously low.

CHAPTER 7

Economy and Income

The UK is one of the world's leading economies with the fourth largest gross national product. Its economy took a long time to recover, however, from the devastating effects of World War II, and it was not until the 1990s that it showed significant improvement. The economy was helped partly by membership in the EEC (later, EU), which it joined in 1973. Today, more than half the UK's trade in goods is with other members of the EU.

Between 1995 and 2005, the UK economy grew at a faster rate than many other top industrial nations. Unemployment and inflation both remained low, in stark contrast to economic problems of the 1970s and 1980s. London's role as a global financial center has helped greatly, as has the fact that American and Japanese companies frequently choose the UK as a European base for their factories and offices.

MANUFACTURING

During the 1970s, British manufacturing productivity and competitiveness declined. In the following decade, the Conservative government privatized the UK's heavy industries, including car, truck, and aircraft building, and steel production. Private ownership improved profitability at the expense of jobs and output. Today, the UK's manufacturing sector amounts to just 20 percent of the national economy, compared to about 40 percent in 1945. It brings in more than U.S.$260,557,500,000 per year and employs four million people, or about 14 percent of the workforce.

The UK's most significant manufacturing industries are engineering, food and drink, tobacco, chemicals, paper, printing, metals, minerals, clothing, and footwear. The fastest-growing industries are pharmaceuticals and electrical engineering.

◀ Since the 1980s, London's Docklands area has been transformed into a major financial center, with many of the world's banks opening offices there.

Investment by foreign companies has boosted employment in a number of UK regions. This production line worker is employed at a factory near Derby that is owned by the Japanese car manufacturer, Toyota.

? Did you know?

London has more foreign banks than any other city in the world.

Economic data

- Gross National Income (GNI) in U.S.$: 2,016,393,000,000
- World rank by GNI: 4
- GNI per capita in U.S.$: 33,940
- World rank by GNI per capita: 13
- Economic growth: 2.0%

Source: World Bank

Focus on: Liverpool

With its large port and its location in northwest England, the city of Liverpool played a key role in the growth of UK trade with the Americas and the West Indies in the eighteenth century. The city expanded to become the center of the UK's shipping industry in the nineteenth century, with 7 miles (11 km) of docks. By the mid-twentieth century, however, Liverpool faced decline as Britain's colonial power faded and it struggled to recover from two world wars. Under-investment made matters worse, and thousands of dock workers found themselves unemployed. In the 2000s, the city's economic life was revived thanks to tourism and a city-center regeneration plan. In 2003, Liverpudlians celebrated as their city was named the European Capital of Culture for 2008.

Container ships are loaded with box-car sized containers of goods at Southampton port on the south coast of England. Around 55,000 UK companies export their products around the world.

THE SERVICE SECTOR

In contrast to manufacturing, the UK's service sector has flourished since the 1980s. Today, service industries contribute about 72 percent of the national economy and employ about 75 percent of the workforce. The areas of greatest growth are banking, insurance, and business support (which includes computing, advertising, and market research). With its many historic buildings, theaters, museums, and picturesque countryside, the UK also has a thriving tourist industry. Every year, about 24 million tourists visit the UK, spending over U.S.$17 billion.

TRADE

The UK economy has long been dependent on trade with foreign nations. Its farms only produce two-thirds of the food needed to feed its population, and it also must import many of the raw materials it needs for its manufacturing. The total value of the UK's foreign trade (imports and exports) is nearly half the nation's gross domestic product. (The equivalent figure for the U.S. is just one fifth.) Major UK exports include machinery, cars, electronic equipment, chemicals, oil, and financial services.

Half of all UK trade is with EU countries, although its single largest export market and second largest supplier is the U.S. Its largest supplier and second largest export market is Germany. Since 1985 (apart from a brief period in the late 1990s), the UK has had a balance of trade deficit, meaning that it imports more goods than it exports.

? Did you know?

UK employers are not allowed to make their staff work longer than forty-eight hours per week. Nonetheless, the UK still has one of the longest working weeks in Europe. Employees in France and Spain don't have to work longer than thirty-eight to forty hours per week.

THE WORKFORCE

About thirty million people work in the UK today—about half the total population. A small but growing proportion of these (13 percent in 2004) are self-employed. One fifth of the self-employed people in the UK work in construction. Most others work in sales, catering, finance, or insurance.

Today, women account for 47 percent of the workforce, compared to 32 percent in 1959. The changing role of women in the UK has led to far more women pursuing careers than they did in the 1950s. Men and women still generally work in different fields, however, with about a quarter of the women doing administrative or secretarial work, while men are more likely to be managers or working in skilled trades.

THE NORTH-SOUTH DIVIDE

The availability of jobs is not evenly distributed around the UK. People living in the south are likely to be better educated and earn more than those in the north. In 2004, the average weekly wage in the north-east of England was U.S.$654, compared to U.S.$791 in the southeast (although admittedly prices are also higher in the southeast).

Between 1991 and 2001, the UK experienced a large migration of skilled workers, with half a million moving from north to south because of greater job opportunities in southern Britain, especially in London. Over 1.7 million jobs were created in London's financial sector during this period, while the northern cities of Glasgow, Liverpool, and Manchester suffered population declines of 8 to 10 percent.

▲ Properties display *for sale* signs in fashionable Brighton, on England's south coast.

▲ Economy by sector

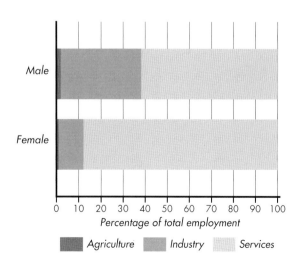

▲ Labor force by sector and gender

CHAPTER 8

Global Connections

As an island nation with a strong seafaring tradition, the United Kingdom has always had an international outlook. Helped by its historical and cultural ties with the former colonies of its empire, and by its proximity to continental Europe, the UK remains a major global player and influential member of several leading international organizations.

During its imperial heyday, the UK influenced its colonies in many ways, introducing British systems of administration, law, and education, as well as British customs and sports. Perhaps the most important legacy of the British Empire is the English language, which today is spoken by about 380 million people as a first language, and is the most widely learned second language in the world. It is also the global "lingua franca," or language used to conduct business.

THE COMMONWEALTH

As the British Empire began to fall apart in the first half of the 20th century, it reorganized. A Commonwealth was established consisting of the UK, many of its former colonies, and two countries that had not been colonies, Cameroon and Mozambique. The Commonwealth has fifty-three member nations, and, although the British monarch remains its formal head, all the member nations are politically independent of the UK. The heads of government of the member nations meet every two years to discuss matters of common interest.

The aims of the Commonwealth are to promote democracy, good government, human rights, and economic development. For example, in the 1980s, the Commonwealth imposed political and moral sanctions on apartheid in South Africa. This

▶ The opening ceremony at the 2002 Commonwealth Games in Manchester. The role of these games, held every four years, is to strengthen the bonds between member nations and encourage sport and physical recreation throughout the Commonwealth.

was one of several factors that helped to bring about the end of apartheid in the early 1990s. In 2002, the Commonwealth suspended Zimbabwe because of the violence and intimidation of the Zimbabwean government against some of its own people. Admittedly, this action has yet to effect any positive change in Zimbabwe.

GROUP OF EIGHT

The UK is a member of the Group of Eight (or G8), an organization of the eight major industrialized democracies. The UK government has an opportunity to air its views and try to reach international agreement on a range of economic and political issues at the annual G8 summit conference. Topics for debate include arms control, economic development, international terrorism, and world health. The 2005 G8 summit, held at Gleneagles, north of Edinburgh in Scotland, resulted in some important agreements covering development in Africa and tackling climate change.

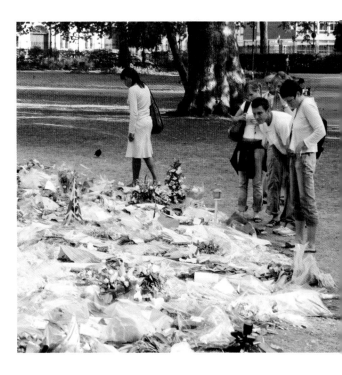

▲ Floral tributes left at the scene of one of the terrorist bomb attacks on London, which occurred on July 7, 2005. The attacks were timed to coincide with the G8 summit.

Focus on: Hong Kong

In 1898, China leased the island of Hong Kong, on its southern coast, to the UK for 99 years. In 1997, as demanded by the terms of the lease, the UK handed back control of the island to China. Many residents of Hong Kong were concerned that China, with its communist policies, would wish to change the island's free-enterprise economy. China, however, has allowed Hong Kong to continue with its capitalist economic system and granted it some political autonomy.

Focus on: Overseas Territories

Remnants of the once-mighty British Empire remain in the form of UK overseas territories (formerly known as dependent territories). These include the Falkland Islands, Montserrat, Gibraltar, the Cayman Islands, the Pitcairn Islands and the British Virgin Islands. Most overseas territories were at one time directly administered by officials appointed by the British government. Today, however, most are self-governing colonies, with their own legislatures, only depending on the UK for defense, foreign affairs, and some trade issues.

THE EUROPEAN UNION

Since 1973, the UK has been a member of the EU (formerly the EEC until 1993). Being part of this single market with Europe—the largest single market in the world—has greatly benefited the UK economy. It has also given UK citizens the right to travel and work throughout Europe. EU membership gives the UK the opportunity to act in concert with other European nations on matters of international concern such as crime, terrorism, immigration, and environmental protection.

On the other hand, the UK's geographical position as an island on the edge of continental Europe and its historic rivalry with several European nations have served to give it a slightly distanced relationship with the EU. The UK decided not to join twelve other EU members in adopting a single currency, the Euro, in 2000, and many in the UK distrust the growing power of the EU to make decisions that affect the lives of British people. For example, European Union directives have made the use of metric weights and measures compulsory throughout the EU. This shift has caused some anger among traders and members of the public in Britain, where traditional imperial measures are still widely used.

THE UNITED NATIONS

Founded in 1945, the UN is an organization that works for world peace and security. The UK is one of only five permanent members of the UN Security Council. The other four are the U.S., France, Russia, and China. This body has the power to decide what action the UN should take in order to solve international conflicts. The UK was the first of the permanent members to make its armed forces and police available to the UN for peacekeeping operations, and it has since played a major role in UN operations around the globe, for example, there are nearly 400 British troops in the UN peacekeeping force in Cyprus.

▶ A British member of the UN peacekeeping force helps guard the buffer zone between the Turkish and Greek communities on the island of Cyprus.

NATO

The UK was a founding member of NATO, a military alliance of twenty nations in North America and Europe. It was originally established in 1949 during the Cold War with the USSR and its allies (1945–1990). Since the end of the Cold War, NATO's main roles have been resolving conflicts, peacekeeping, and fighting terrorism. In the early 21st century, the UK was involved in all four of NATO's major operations. These involved security operations in Afghanistan, Iraq, and the Balkans, and an anti-terrorist operation in the Mediterranean called Operation Active Endeavour which began in 2001 and is still continuing.

Focus on: The Special Relationship

Since joining forces to defeat the Nazis and Fascists in World War II, the UK and the U.S. have been very close political allies. Their shared cultural heritage has generally given the two countries a similar outlook on world events, and the UK has been traditionally very supportive of the U.S. This "special relationship" with the world's only superpower has been very advantageous to the UK. It does sometimes cause problems, however, for example when the British government supported the 2003 U.S.-led invasion of Iraq, which provoked great popular opposition in Britain.

▲ U.S. President George W. Bush (*left*) at a press conference with Tony Blair, the British Prime Minister.

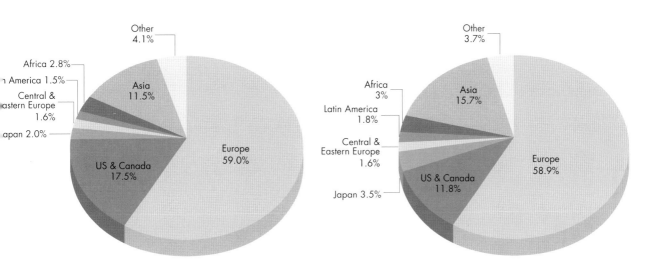

▲ Destination of UK exports by major trading region

▲ Origin of UK imports by major trading region

Transportation and Communications

Historically, the UK led the world in the development of various forms of transportation, including shipping, rail, and aviation. Today, the dominant mode of transportation in the UK is the car.

SHIPPING

The UK has long had a significant shipping industry. The irregular coastline of the British Isles provides it with plenty of natural harbors, and it also has many navigable rivers. The UK has a large merchant fleet that carries freight to and from the nation's eighty commercial ports, while passenger ships regularly ferry people to and from the European mainland and Ireland. The UK also has a network of inland waterways on which it transports goods and where people enjoy recreational boating.

▼ Private toll roads, such as the M6 toll road in the West Midlands, attempt to combat road congestion.

ROADS

For its size, the UK has a large road network, with around 244,000 miles (393,000 km) of roads, including 2,113 miles (3,400 km) of highways. Road transportation is by far the most common form of travel in the UK today. About 65 percent of freight is carried on roads, and about 90 percent of all passenger travel is by road, and most of that is by private car. The growth in private car ownership is one of the most significant developments in the UK's recent transportation history. Between 1980 and 2004, the number of private vehicles increased by 41 percent. Today, 74 percent of UK households own at least one car and pay a tax on each vehicle. Road traffic increased by 71 percent between 1980 and 2000. Motorists' pressure groups continually push the government to build more highways, especially in the southeast. Government concerns about the road congestion and pollution caused by excessive car use has led them to try to tempt more people to use public transportation by raising taxes on fuel. Between 1975 and 2000, fuel tax revenues rose by almost U.S.$42 billion, making UK gasoline the most expensive in Europe. These costs led to fuel tax protests in 2000, which discouraged the government from implementing any further tax increases since then.

▲ Streetcars, called *trams*, in the center of Nottingham—the latest of seven UK cities that have introduced tram systems, since 1980, to deal with congestion. Trams run on rails and are powered by electricity from overhead wires.

RAILWAYS

In the 19th century, the UK developed the world's first rail network. From the mid-1950s, a modernization program began and steam trains were replaced by diesel and electric ones. In the late 1960s, competition from the roads began to take effect, and many less profitable branch lines were closed. In the early 21st century, the number of passenger trips once again approached the levels of the 1950s, although rail had a far smaller share of overall travel. As part of the government's policy to boost train use, there has been significant investment in the West Coast Main Line, which runs between London and Glasgow, with diverging routes to many other British towns and cities. The West Coast Route Modernization program will involve renewal and modernization of some 1,660 miles (2672 km) of track, including around 10,000 bridges and 2,800 signals.

Focus on: The Channel Tunnel

In 1994, the UK was linked to mainland Europe—for the first time since the Ice Age—by a rail tunnel built underneath the English Channel. The Channel Tunnel is 31 miles (50 km) in length and runs from Folkestone, England, to Calais, France, at an average depth of 131 feet (40 m) below the sea bed. By 2000, the tunnel's trains were carrying half the car traffic between Dover or Folkstone and Calais.

 Did you know?

Today's UK rail network includes 10,734 miles (17,274 km) of railway track, over 2,500 stations, and 40,000 bridges and tunnels.

Several British cities have their own rail networks. The largest is the London Underground—the oldest underground railway in the world. Today, London Underground has 408 km (253 miles) of railway and 275 stations, and carries three million passengers per day.

AIR TRAVEL

The UK commercial aviation industry has experienced phenomenal growth since its early days in the mid-20th century. The number of passengers using UK airports rose from three million in 1953 to 200 million in 2003. British Airways, the UK's biggest airline, operates the world's largest network of flights, travelling to over 550 destinations in nearly 90 countries around the world. London's main airports, Heathrow and Gatwick, are among the world's busiest. In 2003, 63 million passengers used Heathrow, and 30 million passed through Gatwick.

TELECOMMUNICATIONS

The UK has one of the most advanced telecommunications systems in the world. In the 1990s and 2000s, the largest telephone service provider, British Telecom, faced increasing competition from other providers. The service evolved rapidly in the 1990s with advances in cellular phones and the development of email, the Internet, and wireless technology. By the end of 2004, there were over 60 million cell phones in the UK, and about 2.5 million subscribers to the latest generation of cell phones, 3G. These can carry a lot more information, and therefore can be used for more applications than simple phone calls, such as TV, computer, and email.

▼ Today, nearly 90 percent of UK citizens between ages 15 and 34 own a cell phone. Many use them for text messaging as much as for speaking.

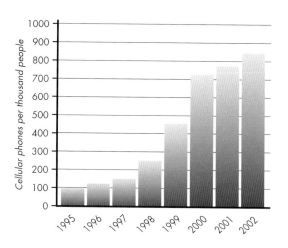

▲ Cell phone use, 1995–2002

◀ A row of terraced houses with satellite dishes. Satellite television companies have grabbed an ever-larger share of UK TV audiences, largely because of their exclusive broadcasts of popular sports and movies.

People in the UK have taken on the new technologies at a startling rate. By the end of 2004, six million (or nearly 30 percent) of British homes were connected to broadband, an increase of 90 percent from 2003. By March 2005, 62 percent of UK homes had digital TV, and consumers had a choice of over 370 TV channels. These developments are affecting the way people live, with increasing numbers using the technology to work and shop from home.

Transport & communications data

- Total roads: 244,163 miles/392,931 km
- Total paved roads: 244,163 miles/ 392,931 km
- Total unpaved roads: 0 miles/0 km
- Total railways: 10,734 miles/17,274 km
- Major airports: 471
- Cars per 1,000 people: 384
- Cell phones per 1,000 people: 841
- Personal computers per 1,000 people: 406
- Internet users per 1,000 people: 423

Source: World Bank and CIA World Factbook

Did you know?

The UK has 148 civil airfields, 13 of which can handle more than a million passengers each.

Focus on: The Press

More people read newspapers in the UK than in almost any other developed nation. Around 60 percent of adult citizens read a daily paper and more than 65 percent buy a Sunday paper. To service this appetite, the UK has a large and diverse range of newspapers, with ten morning dailies and nine Sunday papers published nationally. These range from "quality" newspapers with news and current affairs to the "tabloids," which offer a mix of news, gossip, and entertainment. The UK also has 1,400 regional and local papers and more than 6,500 magazines.

CHAPTER 10

Education and Health

Education is vital in a developed economy such as the UK, which depends on a regular workforce of educated professionals and skilled workers. The UK has one of the world's highest university graduation rates, with 36 percent of the population achieving a first degree. It also has two world-renowned universities—Oxford and Cambridge.

SCHOOLS

All children in the UK receive compulsory primary and secondary education from age five up to age sixteen. Children attend primary school until eleven, and then go to secondary school.

▼ Pupils carry out a science experiment at a comprehensive school. Comprehensive schools admit pupils regardless of ability or social background.

Secondary schools are either publicly funded and offer free education, or they are funded by fee-paying students (known as independent schools). The vast majority of students (95 percent) go to publicly funded schools. Most of these are "comprehensive schools," which offer all types of secondary education and do not select their pupils. Other types of publicly funded school include specialist schools, which focus on particular subjects like the arts or sports, and grammar schools, which select all or most of their students and offer a more academic syllabus.

Since 1988, UK schools have followed the National Curriculum, designed to raise standards and set attainment targets for learning. The Curriculum has been criticized by some for restricting teachers' freedom and giving too little time for certain subjects. At sixteen, all pupils take exams called GCSEs (General Certificate of Secondary Education). Pupils can then decide whether to continue their education or seek employment. About one third leave education at this stage. Those who continue can study for Advanced Level exams at eighteen and apply to go to university or go to a college to gain vocational skills.

UNIVERSITIES

There are over ninety universities in the UK. The most famous of these are Oxford and Cambridge, both founded in the Middle Ages. Until 1998, the government paid university students a grant to help them with their costs. In the 1990s, universities faced a funding crisis and the government replaced the grant with a loan to be repaid after graduation. Students were also asked to pay a proportion of their tuition fees. In the early 2000s, universities still faced financial difficulties and several were forced to close down departments. A new law, passed in 2004, introduced "top-up fees," which allowed universities to set their own tuition fees up to a cap of about U.S.$5,000 per year. Some felt that would give students too much debt and stop many from going on to higher education. The impact of these costs remains to be seen.

▼ The Bridge of Sighs, one of Oxford University's most famous landmarks, joins two sections of Hertford College, whose former students include the writers John Donne, Jonathan Swift, and Evelyn Waugh.

 Did you know?

In 1960–1961, women made up only a quarter of full-time university students in the UK. By 2002–2003, 54 percent of university undergraduates were female.

Education and health

- Life expectancy at birth, male: 75.2
- Life expectancy at birth, female: 80.1
- Infant mortality rate per 1,000: 5
- Under five mortality rate per 1,000: 6
- Physicians per 1,000 people: 2.1
- Health expenditure as % of GDP: 7.7
- Education expenditure as % of GDP: 4.7
- Primary net enrollment: 100%
- Pupil-teacher ratio, primary school: 17.2
- Adult literacy as % age 15+: 99.0

Source: United Nations Agencies and World Bank

HEALTH

Like most developed countries, the UK has enjoyed substantial gains in the health of its population over the past forty years. In 2003, life expectancy at birth in the UK was 77.6 years, almost eight years higher than it was in 1960, and about 0.7 years higher than average for an economically developed country. The infant mortality rate in the UK in 2003 was 5.3 deaths per 1,000 live births—lower than most developed countries, although higher than the EU average. By contrast, in 2004 the U.S. infant mortality rate had risen to 7 per 1,000 live births.

The number of adult smokers in the UK has declined sharply. In 2003, 26 percent of the adult population smoked compared to 40 percent in 1978. At the same time, the UK has seen a dramatic rise in obesity. Today, about 20 percent of the UK population is obese, three times as many as in 1983. Increased obesity is already leading to increases in health problems such as diabetes, asthma, and heart disease. The government has responded to this problem with various steps. For example, food manufacturers have been urged to reduce levels of sugar and salt in their products, and schools are to provide healthier meals and more physical exercise for their pupils.

THE NATIONAL HEALTH SERVICE

In 1948, a National Health Service (NHS) was established in the UK. It provided free medical care for all British citizens, regardless of their income, paid for out of taxation. The NHS of today, however, is quite different from the vision of its founders. The service now charges for items such as prescriptions, dentures, and eyeglasses. Furthermore, since 1990, the NHS has undergone various reforms by governments concerned about its rising costs and inefficiency.

In the 1990s, the Conservative government tried to increase efficiency by introducing an internal market, by which hospitals were turned into trusts and given the power to determine how they spent government funds. Many general practitioners (GPs) were given budgets to buy health care from these trusts in a plan called GP fund holding. This system was criticized for causing a "two-tier" health service, with GP fund holders able to obtain treatment quicker than non-fund holders.

◀ The government-sponsored five-a-day campaign encourages people to eat at least five portions of fruit and vegetables every day. As part of the national campaign, all four- to six-year olds are entitled to a free piece of fruit or a vegetable each school day.

▶ A young patient has her plaster cast removed by an NHS nurse. Despite recent reforms, the NHS remains the most government-funded health care service in the Western world, with only 5 percent of NHS revenue coming from charges.

Starting in 1998, the Labour government abolished the internal market and began introducing a series of new reforms. These included targets for increasing the numbers of hospitals, doctors, and nurses, and reducing hospital waiting lists. They also reorganized the NHS structure, giving locally based organizations called Primary Care Trusts the power to run NHS services in their area. In 2000, the government also pledged to increase public spending on health by 7 percent per year for five years, starting in 2002, to bring it into line with other European countries. The additional funding has had mixed results. Waiting lists fell from 1.16 million in 1997 to 850,000 in September 2004. At the same time, the UK continues to have one of the highest death rates in Europe for the "superbugs," cancer and heart disease. As part of the government's plan to reduce NHS waiting lists, some NHS trusts have set up agreements with private healthcare providers to offer NHS patients treatment in a private hospital at no charge to the patient. Some politicians and health professionals fear that this may lead to an increasing privatization of the NHS.

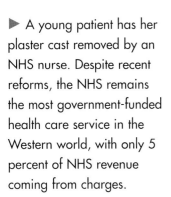

▲ Life expectancy at birth 1960-2003

? Did you know?

The NHS is the largest organization in Europe, employing around 1.2 million staff and with an annual budget of about U.S.$85 billion.

CHAPTER 11

Culture and Religion

The UK is a country of diverse cultures and traditions. Although English culture tends to dominate, each region of the UK—Wales, Scotland, and Northern Ireland—maintains its own unique customs, cuisine, and festivals. Since the 1950s, immigrants from the UK's former colonies have brought Afro-Caribbean and Asian cultures to the UK.

THE ARTS

Over the centuries, the UK has produced many fine artists, writers, and musicians who have made their mark around the globe. The plays of William Shakespeare have enriched the English language and are performed in every part of the world. The 18th century English writers Daniel Defoe and Samuel Richardson pioneered the novel, which was taken to new heights by authors such as Jane Austen, Charles Dickens, and the Brontë sisters. The poet Geoffrey Chaucer brought an earthy realism to depictions of medieval life, while William Wordsworth tried to bring poetic language closer to natural speech. The English landscape painter, J.M.W. Turner, well known for his dramatic treatment of natural light, influenced the development of impressionist painters such as Pissarro, Monet, and Sisley. The writer J.K. Rowling now thrills a whole generation of children with her unique Harry Potter adventures.

In the 20th century, the UK's main contributions to world culture have been in the fields of popular music, fashion, and film. In the 1960s, the Beatles and the Rolling Stones were the first British bands to win international followings, while London became known as a leader of fashion with the brightly

◀ The Beatles arrive in the U.S. on one of their sell-out tours. In August 1965, this Liverpudlian band played before a record-breaking 55,600 people at New York's Shea Stadium.

colored outfits being sold in Carnaby Street and the King's Road. Since the 1960s, British filmmakers such as Ken Loach and Mike Leigh have gained international respect for their portrayals of ordinary British life in movies such as *Kes* (1969) and *Life is Sweet* (1990).

FOOD AND DRINK

A traditional British meal consists of meat accompanied by potatoes and one (or more) other vegetable. Perhaps the most famous British dish is roast beef and Yorkshire pudding. Other favorites include shepherd's pie, fish and chips, and (originating in the southwest) Cornish pasties and scones with clotted cream. The most popular hot drink is tea. Adults also enjoy drinking beer in pubs (bars). Bars selling wine are also increasingly popular among citydwellers. Since the 1950s, British cuisine has changed, due to foreign influences. Popular meals today include pizzas, hamburgers, and Chinese and Indian food.

Focus on: The Edinburgh Fringe

Every year in late summer, the city of Edinburgh, Scotland, hosts an international arts festival. Alongside the official festival, there is a "Fringe" festival that offers opportunities to all performers and therefore tends to attract more unconventional acts. The Edinburgh Fringe includes a mix of theater, comedy, and music. It began when too many performers turned up to the first Edinburgh Festival in 1947. Those who were excluded formed their own festival. In 2005, the Fringe presented almost 27,000 performances of 1,800 shows, and sold 1.25 million tickets.

▼ Every year at the Fringe, street performers entertain festival-goers on Edinburgh's Royal Mile.

CHRISTIAN WORSHIP

Since Henry VIII's split with the Roman Catholic Church in the 16th century, the UK has officially been a Protestant country. The national Churches in the UK are the Church of England (or Anglican Church) and the Church of Scotland (or Presbyterian Church). The Churches in Wales and Northern Ireland are part of the Anglican Communion, meaning that they recognize the authority of the Anglican Church.

Further splits in the Church of England in the 17th century led to the founding of "Nonconformist" Churches such as the Baptists and Congregationalists, who desired simpler forms of worship. The Methodist Church was founded in the 18th century as part of a religious revival centered in the industrial northeast, where it remains strong. The Presbyterian Church of Wales, closely linked with Welsh culture and language, was founded in the 18th century and is still a significant religious body in that region.

There are around 49.5 million Christians in the UK, including 5.6 million Catholics. This represents almost 83 percent of the population. Very few British Christians actually attend church, however, except for baptisms, weddings, and funerals. Around a million people attend Anglican churches each Sunday.

OTHER RELIGIOUS GROUPS

Although the official religion of the UK is Protestantism, it is a country of religious freedom, and people are allowed to practice whatever faith they like without interference from the government. Catholics have continued living in the UK since the Reformation, Jews have settled in the UK since the 17th century, and other non-Christian communities have grown in numbers since the immigration of the 1950s. Currently, Muslims, Hindus, Jews, Sikhs, and Buddhists make up the bulk of non-Christian religious groups living in the UK.

◀ A bride and groom are showered with confetti at a traditional church wedding in Cllitheroe, Lancashire. About a third of all weddings in Britain are performed in an Anglican church.

◀ A congregation gather at a British mosque in Preston, Lancashire, for Friday prayers. Every year, around 20,000 British Muslims travel to Mecca for the Hajj, which is an annual religious pilgrimage.

RELIGIOUS TENSIONS

Because of the UK's tradition of tolerance, the country has suffered relatively little religious tension. One of the few places where religion and politics are still strongly connected is Northern Ireland. Here, the Protestant majority of the north wish to maintain the political union with the UK, while the Roman Catholic minority support union with Ireland. This long-running conflict blew up into thirty years of violent troubles, beginning in 1969.

Another, more recent, source of tension has emerged with the rise of militant fundamentalists within the Muslim community,

partly inflamed by the UK's role in the war against Iraq. On July 7, 2005, a group of militant Islamists set off bombs in central London, killing fifty-six people. Another set of attacks was attempted two weeks later, but mercifully failed. Since then, the government has acted to ban certain extremist organizations and to deport a number of radical preachers.

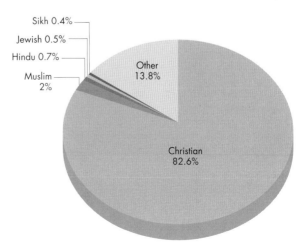

Sikh 0.4%
Jewish 0.5%
Hindu 0.7%
Muslim 2%
Other 13.8%
Christian 82.6%

▲ The United Kingdom's major religions

 Did you know?

The UK has one of the largest Muslim communities in Western Europe, and over 600 mosques and prayer centers. One of the most important Muslim institutions in the Western world is the Central Mosque in London.

CHAPTER 12

Leisure and Tourism

People in the UK work an average of 44.8 hours per week and receive an average of between four and five weeks of vacation per year. In addition, they have days off around the major holidays of Christmas, New Year, and Easter, and there are three extra "bank holidays" in May and August.

LEISURE PURSUITS

The most popular leisure activities in the UK are watching television and listening to music or the radio. An average of three hours per day are spent watching TV. While 99 percent of British people watch television, just 65 percent read books.

Cinema is another favorite pastime. The British public made 171 million visits to UK cinemas in 2004, making the UK second highest in Europe, after France, for cinema attendance. Theaters, museums, and art galleries also enjoy popularity, with 24 percent of the population attending.

KEEPING ACTIVE

The British are also great sports enthusiasts— both watching and playing it. About 59 percent of adults take part in some regular sport, exercise, or outdoor pursuit. The most popular are walking, swimming, aerobic exercise, yoga, cycling, and a kind of pool called snooker. Nearly 10 percent of the population are members of health clubs, leisure centers, or gyms. Fishing, climbing, sailing, and bird watching are also common outdoor pursuits. Another favorite activity is gardening—about half the families in the UK maintain a garden.

The most popular spectator sport is soccer, called football. Every Saturday during the football season, thousands of fans attend

▼ Hiking, or rambling, is a highly popular activity in the UK. The Ramblers' Association has almost 140,000 members in England, Scotland, and Wales.

◄ Players from Scotland's two biggest soccer teams, Celtic (*green and white stripes*) and Rangers, tussle for the ball.

matches in every town and city in the country. Several of the top British football clubs, such as Manchester United and Liverpool, are world famous. Other popular spectator sports include rugby, cricket, track and field athletics, and horse racing. Tennis becomes briefly popular for two weeks each summer during the international Wimbledon Championships.

Since the 1990s, sports have declined in British schools. Schools' increased emphasis on teaching children literacy and mathematics has meant less time for physical education and sports. School playing fields have been sold off to local councils and private developers. The government has tried to reverse this trend by developing specialist sports schools, bringing coaching specialists into schools, and encouraging high-profile sports stars to make school visits. The status of sports is likely to grow in UK schools, because London has been awarded the 2012 Olympic Games.

Focus on: The London Marathon

The London Marathon, which takes place each year in April, is the world's largest marathon, attracting over 100,000 applications for the 20,000 available places. A further 25,000 places in the race are reserved for charity runners.

Participants run the 26.2-mile course from Greenwich Park in southeast London to the Mall and Buckingham Palace. Over 375,000 spectators line the route. Each year, the marathon raises about U.S.$52 million for charity.

▲ The goal of the Eden Project in Cornwall, one of the UK's top tourist attractions, is to promote understanding of the natural world. Its domes are "biomes," with controlled climates that house plants from tropical and temperate regions.

TOURISM IN THE UK

The UK tourist industry has grown dramatically in recent years, with the number of foreign visitors doubling between 1983 and 2003 from about 12 million to 24 million. The majority of tourists are from Europe, with 16 million visitors in 2003—four times the number from North America. Most tourist trips in the UK, however, are made by UK residents. For example, in 2002, 167.3 million tourist visits were made to different parts of the UK by British residents—87.3 percent of the total.

The United Kingdom offers about 6,400 major tourist attractions, including museums, art galleries, wildlife centers, historic houses and castles, churches and cathedrals, gardens, and leisure parks. In 2001, these received a total of 452 million visits. Popular attractions include (not in order of popularity): Blackpool Pleasure Beach in Lancashire, Brighton Pier, the Eden Project in Cornwall, the Lake District in Cumbria, Hadrian's Wall in Northumbria, Snowdonia in Wales, the Peak District National Park, and Edinburgh Castle in Scotland.

By far the most popular destination for overseas tourists is London, which received 11.7 million visitors in 2003. Many come to see the capital city's world-famous sights, its galleries, and incredible museums. Top attractions (based on visitor numbers) include the Tower of London, the National Gallery, the British Museum—which houses tremendous collections and wonders, including the Rosetta Stone, Egyptian sphinxes, and rare books—the London Eye (the largest observation wheel in the world), and the Tate Modern, an art museum.

In total, the UK tourist industry is worth approximately U.S.$278 billion per year—around six percent of the gross domestic product. In fact, it is growing—about one in five of all new jobs created in the UK since 1997 have been in the tourist industry. Foreign tourists, however, still spend about U.S.$8 billion less in the UK than British tourists spend abroad.

HOLIDAYS ABROAD

Taking vacations overseas has become a lot cheaper in recent decades, with the emergence of package holidays and low-cost airlines. This change has led to a huge growth in the number of Britons taking foreign vacations. UK residents made a record 41.2 million vacation trips abroad in 2003, compared to just 6.7 million foreign vacations in 1971. Almost half the trips taken in 2003 were vacation packages.

Since 1994, the favorite destination for British vacationers has been Spain, which was the venue for 30 percent of all UK foreign vacations in 2003. The next most popular destination was France, with 18 percent. In fact, nine out of the ten most frequently visited countries are in the EU. The exception is the U.S., which attracted five percent of all vacationers.

▲ The London Eye takes people above the London skyline, giving them spectacular views of up to 25 miles across the city and beyond, including St. Paul's, the Palace of Westminster, and Windsor Castle.

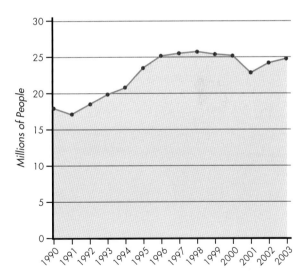

▲ Changes in international tourism, 1990-2002

Tourism in The United Kingdom

▱ Tourist arrivals, millions: 24.785

▱ Earnings from tourism in U.S.$: 30,656,000,000

▱ Tourism as % foreign earnings: 7.0

▱ Tourist departures, millions: 61.453

▱ Expenditure on tourism in U.S.$: 58,602,000,384

Source: World Bank

 Did you know?

The UK is the fifth most popular vacation destination in the world, after the United States, Italy, France, and Spain.

CHAPTER 13

Environment and Conservation

There is mounting scientific evidence of the negative effect of human consumption patterns on the environment. In the UK, this impact can be seen, for example, in the poor air quality of many British cities caused by high levels of road traffic. The UK government, under pressure from environmental activists and concerned citizens, has concluded that current lifestyles must change.

CLIMATE CHANGE

Much of the UK's economic prosperity was built on the use of fossil fuels. Most scientists believe that the emissions of carbon dioxide and other greenhouse gases, caused by burning fossil fuels, are starting to change the world's climate. In 1997, the UK signed the Kyoto Protocol, legally binding the government to reduce the UK's

greenhouse gas emissions by 12.5 percent below 1990 levels by 2008–2012. In 2000, the UK government set itself an even tougher target of cutting carbon dioxide emissions by 20 percent below 1990 levels by 2010.

To achieve these targets, the government planned a campaign to change public attitudes and try to promote better energy efficiency at home and at work. Other measures included cutting emissions from road vehicles by encouraging the use of low-emitting cars and buses; increasing the proportion of UK electricity produced from renewable energy

▼ This zero-emissions car at Sussex University illustrates the potential for a more environmentally friendly future for British road vehicles.

sources to 10 percent by 2010; and ensuring that new buildings are more energy efficient. For example, providing better insulation for walls and roofs can prevent heat loss and save on the amount of fuel needed to heat a building. Some progress has been made: greenhouse gas emissions in 2002 were 15 percent below 1990s levels. In 2003, however, just 4 percent of UK electricity was produced from renewable sources, compared to an EU average of 14 percent.

WASTE AND RECYCLING

The environmental impact of waste can be reduced by recycling or composting. Estimates suggest that as much as 60 percent of household waste could be recycled, yet England managed just 17.7 percent in 2003–2004—one of the lowest rates in Europe. Regional differences are marked. In 2001–2002, England's northeast recycled just 136 pounds (62 kilograms) per household per year, while households in the southeast averaged 488 lb (222 kg) per year. The government hopes to increase the amount of recycled waste to 25 percent in 2005 and 33 percent by 2015. To meet these targets, they plan to provide curbside recycling collection to every household in the country.

POLLUTION

As an industrialized nation, pollution of air and water has been a problem in the UK since the 19th century. Since the Clean Air Acts of 1956 and 1968 banned coal burning in urban areas,

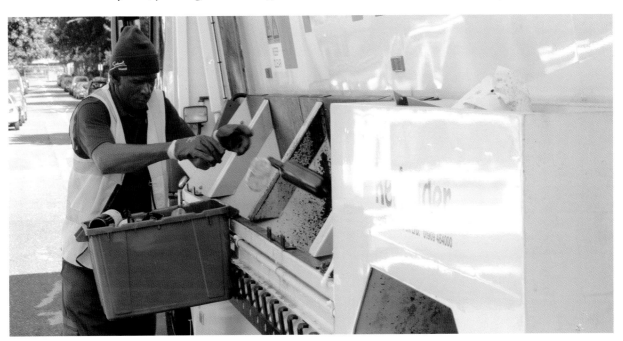

▲ Recycled waste being collected from people's curbsides in London. The government and the local authorities have embarked on a campaign to persuade more people to recycle more of their household waste.

 Did you know?

The UK produces well over 98 million tons (100 million tonnes) of industrial and domestic waste annually, and this quantity is growing by three percent every year.

emissions of sulphur dioxide and smoke have fallen dramatically. In the 1980s, the UK signed international protocols to reduce emissions of nitrogen oxides that cause acid rain. Emissions in the UK fell by 44 percent between 1990 and 2003 to 1545 tons (1,570 tonnes).

Discharges from industry, agriculture, and sewage treatment works have hurt UK's rivers. Since 1990, however, the water companies have spent about U.S.$10 billion cleaning up Britain's rivers, and they plan to spend a further U.S.$3.5 billion by 2010. This effort has brought some improvements, with 65 percent of rivers achieving good quality ratings in 2004, which is 17 percent better than in 1990.

▼ A volunteer helps clear trash from the Wandle River in London. The Wandle was once a highly polluted river that has recently been cleaned up.

WILDLIFE CONSERVATION

Wildlife has suffered numerous threats in the UK over the past hundred years. Problems include habitat loss, caused, for example, by farmers draining wetlands for agriculture and allowing overgrazing on upland moors. Another threat comes from the introduction of nonnative species that eat— or out-compete— native species. For example, the gray squirrel, introduced in the 1800s, is thought to have caused a decline in the native red squirrel population. Pollution also damages sensitive species or ecosystems.

In recent years, the government-funded Environment Agency has worked to improve the UK's biodiversity (the range of living things in a country, region, or ecological system) through Habitat Action Plans, improving forty-five wildlife habitats around the country. The agency has also introduced 391 Species Action Plans to sustain and increase the populations of threatened species, including otters, water voles, southern damselflies, and barn owls.

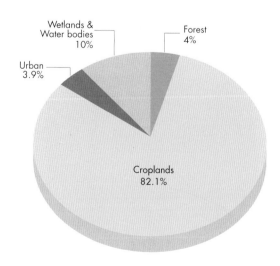

Wetlands & Water bodies 10%

Forest 4%

Urban 3.9%

Croplands 82.1%

▲ Types of habitat

Bird populations are a good indicator of the general health of a country's wildlife. The UK's overall bird population increased by 13 percent between 1970 and 2002, although it had a slight decrease between 2000 and 2002. Successful species include the Dartford warbler. This bird may have benefited from climate change because the warming climate has expanded the area where it can breed in the UK to include more northerly areas. Farmland species such as turtledove and skylark, however, fell by 42 percent between 1970 and 2002, mainly because of intensive farming, which robbed them of some of their habitat. Overgrazing and the concentrated use of fertilizers and insecticides have caused a reduction in the plants and insects on which these birds feed.

▶ The red squirrel is one native species that has become seriously endangered, with only around 160,000 remaining, compared to over 2.5 million gray squirrels.

Environmental and conservation data

🗁 Forested area as % total land area: 4

🗁 Protected area as % total land area: 10.5

🗁 Number of protected areas: 7,191

SPECIES DIVERSITY

Category	Known species	Threatened species
Mammals	50	12
Breeding birds	229	2
Reptiles	15	n/a
Amphibians	12	n/a
Fish	427	3
Plants	1,623	13

Source: World Resources Institute

Focus on: The Wildfowl and Wetlands Trust

Wetlands have been called the kidneys of the natural environment due to their ability to clean pollutants from the water supply. Wetland environments in the UK are protected under international and national law because of their unique biodiversity. Established in 1946 by the artist and conservationist Sir Peter Scott, the Wildfowl and Wetlands Trust has campaigned to conserve and protect the UK's wetland environments. Its aim is to sustain the habitat of migratory wildfowl and to protect the rare and delicate ecosystem that brings benefits to bird and animal life.

CHAPTER 14

Future Challenges

The United Kingdom has enjoyed steady economic growth and relative social and political stability in recent years. The nation also faces a number of challenges, however, including regional economic differences, inter-community tensions, and environmental issues.

NORTH AND SOUTH

The UK's economic success is not felt evenly throughout the country. In some areas of the UK, especially the inner cities, real poverty exists. A wealth gap is also growing between the prosperous southeast and the former industrial centers of the north and northeast. As the southeast has prospered, more and more young people have moved south for jobs. This rapid population growth has led to a major housing shortage in the south and placed pressures on the transportation infrastructure. The government has had some success in attracting businesses back to the north, but more needs to be done to avoid increasing a north-south wealth gap.

TENSIONS BETWEEN COMMUNITIES

The Northern Ireland peace process received a boost in July 2005 when the IRA announced the end of its armed struggle. Hopes were raised that the IRA would decommission its weapons and that the Northern Ireland Assembly would be restored. The centuries-long history of the struggle between loyalists and republicans in this region, however, suggests that full peace and restoration will be difficult to achieve.

The racist attitudes suffered by immigrants in the 1970s have declined, although there are signs that a dislike of foreigners is returning in some cities in the northwest of England, where the far-right British National Party (BNP) has made gains. The BNP exploited public fears about the country being swamped by immigrants and asylum seekers. If such attitudes grow, it may start to hurt the UK's reputation as a liberal and tolerant society.

◀ A new business park, being built in Stafford in the North Midlands, is part of efforts to bridge the north-south economic divide by encouraging business and creating jobs in areas other than the southeast. The countryside is changing dramatically as more business parks are built.

ENVIRONMENTAL CHALLENGES

The UK is engaged in a process of transition from an old-style, energy-inefficient, fossil fuel-based economy to one based on principles of sustainable development. This transition is a long-term project and its success will depend on changing public attitudes as much as government action. The most urgent challenge is to find alternative, cleaner energy sources that will meet UK domestic and industrial needs.

EUROPE

One of the UK's major foreign policy challenges is to decide on its relationship with Europe. The issue of EU membership has divided the British people for many years. The United Kingdom is a fiercely proud and independent nation with a rich history and a distinctive culture. The challenge for the UK is to retain its unique character while also enjoying the economic and political benefits of being part of Europe.

▲ United we stand: Londoners observe a two-minute silence for the victims of the July 7, 2005 London bombings, honoring cooperation among all people and defying those who sought to destroy their way of life.

Today, the United Kingdom continues to be one of the world's leading industrial nations. Its historical links with countries all over the world have given the UK both a strong voice in world affairs and a richly diverse culture. The UK is therefore uniquely placed to benefit from the increasingly global nature of business and society. The UK's elevated status on the world stage, however, can also bring challenges such as war and terrorism. As a modern, industrialized nation, it must take its share of responsibility for pollution and the growing rich-poor divide. Closer to home, the British people must also find ways of balancing economic success with a healthy, sustainable energy lifestyle.

Time Line

c. 6500 B.C. Formation of the island of Great Britain.

55 BC Julius Caesar invades Britain.

43 BC–A.D. 410 Period of the Roman occupation of Britain.

449 Angles, Saxons, and Jutes begin to invade Britain.

c. 490–c. 550 Anglo-Saxon kingdoms established.

787 Viking raids begin.

802 Egbert of Wessex becomes king of all England.

871–899 Alfred the Great, King of Wessex, defends England against the Vikings.

1066 William, Duke of Normandy, defeats Harold II at Hastings, and becomes king of England.

1138–1153 Civil war in England.

1154 Henry II (Henry of Anjou) becomes the first Plantagenet king.

1215 King John signs the Magna Carta.

1337–1453 England fights the Hundred Years' War with France.

1348–1351 The Black Death wipes out a third of Britain's population.

1455–1485 The Wars of the Roses.

1485 Henry VII becomes the first Tudor monarch.

1534 Henry VIII passes the Act of Supremacy, establishing himself as leader of the English Church.

1536–43 Wales is annexed to England.

1558–1603 Reign of Queen Elizabeth I.

1588 England defeats the Spanish Armada.

1605 The Gunpowder Plot to blow up Parliament is foiled.

1642–1649 The English Civil War is fought between supporters of King Charles I and Parliament.

1649–1660 The Commonwealth, established by Oliver Cromwell, briefly replaces the monarchy.

1660 Restoration of the monarchy under Charles II.

1688–1689 The defeat of James II and accession of William I to the English throne ends a threat to English Protestantism.

1707 The Act of Union joins the separate nations of England and Scotland and establishes the nation of Great Britain.

1756–1763 Britain fights the Seven Years' War with France, establishing its supremacy in India and North America.

1783 Britain loses the American War of Independence.

1801 Ireland is annexed to Britain to form the United Kingdom.

1805 Napoléon's fleet is defeated by Nelson at the Battle of Trafalgar.

1815 Napoléon is defeated by Wellington at the Battle of Waterloo.

1837–1901 Reign of Queen Victoria.

1914–1918 World War I.

1921 The partition of Ireland. Ulster remains part of the United Kingdom.

1939–1945 World War II. UK cities are heavily bombed in the Blitz.

The British government establishes the National Health Service.

The Troubles begin in Northern Ireland.

1973 The UK joins the EEC.

1975 The first oil is brought ashore from the North Sea.

1982 The UK fights and wins the Falklands War against Argentina.

1999 Powers are devolved from the UK government to regional assemblies.

2001–2002 British involvement in military attacks against Afghanistan.

2003 British forces take part in the U.S.-led war against Iraq.

2005 Suicide bombers blow themselves up in London, killing fifty-six people.

Glossary

Anglican Communion the churches in communion with, and recognizing the authority of, the Church of England

annexed taken over

asylum seekers people who request permission to live in another nation because they face repression in their own country

balance of trade the difference between the value of imports and exports of a country over a fixed period of time

biodiversity the variety of living things found in a particular environment. A high level of biodiversity helps an environment because it increases the chances that some of the living things can survive external threats, such as natural or human-made disasters

biomass plant and animal material used as a source of food

carbon dioxide emissions discharges of the gas carbon dioxide (CO_2), produced whenever fuel is burned. One of the main "greenhouse gases," CO_2 contributes significantly to global warming

Cold War the conflict between the U.S. and the Soviet Union and their allies, which lasted from 1945 to 1990.

Common Agricultural Policy (CAP) the EU's agricultural policy, intended to provide stable markets and incomes for European farmers

constituency one of the areas into which a country is divided for election purposes

constitution a set of rules by which a country is governed

constitutional monarchy a political system in which the head of state is a monarch (king or queen) ruling to the extent allowed by a constitution

devolve to transfer power from central government to regional governments

ecosystem a group of interdependent plants and animals together with the environment they inhabit and depend on

electoral system the system under which elections are held in a particular country

European Union (EU) an economic and political alliance of European nations

feudalism the system that existed in medieval Europe in which barons were given land by the king in exchange for military service

fossil fuels any carbon-containing fuel, such as coal, natural gas, and oil

glaciers large bodies of slowly advancing or retreating ice and compacted snow

global warming the gradual increase in Earth's average temperature, probably caused by the burning of fossil fuels such as oil

gross domestic product (GDP) the total value of goods and services produced by a nation

gross national product (GNP) the total value of goods and services produced by a nation, including goods and services produced abroad

infrastructure the large-scale public systems, services, and equipment needed for a country to function, including roads and telecommunications

Islamist an extremist Muslim who wishes to enforce fundamentalist Islamic law on society

legislation laws

lingua franca a language used between people who have no other language in common

National Curriculum the framework for teaching and learning across a range of subjects that must be followed by all school-age pupils in the UK

nationalize to transfer a business or industry from private ownership to government control

North Atlantic Treaty Organization (NATO) a military alliance of twenty nations in North America and Europe, established in 1949 during the Cold War with the USSR and its allies

nuclear energy the radioactive energy released by nuclear fission (the splitting of an atomic nucleus into smaller nuclei)

parliament the UK's legislative body where bills are debated and passed into law

partition division

precipitation rain, snow, or hail

privatize to transfer a business or industry from government control to private ownership

Protestant Reformation the 16th century movement in Europe that led to the development of Protestant Churches

sovereignty supreme authority over a nation

subsidies grants from a government to businesses or organizations to help them function

tabloids newspapers that emphasize sensational stories

United Nations (UN) an organization of nations, formed in 1945, which meets regularly to promote peace, security, and international cooperation

wetland marshes, swamps, or other areas of land where the soil near the surface is saturated with water

Further Information

BOOKS TO READ

Bowden, Rob.
Changing Face of the United Kingdom.
Hodder Wayland, 2004.

Bowden, Rob.
United Kingdom. Countries of the World
(series).
Evans Publishing, 2002.

Campbell, Kumari
United Kingdom in Pictures. Visual Geography
(series)
Lerner Publications, 2004.

Ganeri, Anita.
Britain and the British. Focus on Europe (series)
Franklin Watts, 2001.

Hynson, Colin.
The Tower of London. Places in History (series).
World Almanac Library, 2005.

Minnis, Ivan
Governing the UK. A Citizen's Guide (series).
Heinemann Library, 2002.

Oliver, C.
Great Britain. Country File (series)
Franklin Watts, 2001.

Ross, Simon.
United Kingdom. Geography 21 (sereies)
HarperCollins, 1998.

Stacey, Gill.
London. Great Cities of the World (series).
World Almanac Library, 2004.

USEFUL WEB SITES

BBC country profile of the UK
news.bbc.co.uk/1/hi/world/europe/
country_profiles/1038758.stm

BBC time line of British history
www.bbc.co.uk/history/timelines/britain/

British history
www.channel4.com/history

Environmental facts and issues
www.environment-agency.gov.uk

Links to the Young Person's Commonwealth
www.thecommonwealth.org/

Office of the British Prime Minister
www.number_10.gov.uk/

Statistics on UK life
www.statistics.gov.uk/

UK government
www.direct.gov.uk/

UK climate
www.metoffice.com/climate/uk/

Index

Page numbers in **bold** indicate pictures.

About the Author

Alex Woolf studied history and government at Essex University. He has spent over ten years as an editor and writer of children's books on history, geography, and social issues. He lives with his wife and son in Southgate, North London, England.